W9-BWT-872

Frederick County Public Libraries

PURCHASED WITH A
GRANT AWARDED BY

G. Frank Thomas Fund

FREDERICK COUNTY PUBLIC LIBRARIES

21st Century Skills INNOVATION *Library*

From Butterfly Wings to . . . Display Technology

by Josh Gregory

INNOVATIONS FROM NATURE

CHERRY
LAKE
Publishing

Published in the United States of America by Cherry Lake Publishing
Ann Arbor, Michigan
www.cherrylakepublishing.com

Content Adviser: Marjan Eggermont, Senior Instructor, Schulich School of Engineering, Calgary, Alberta, Canada

Reading Adviser: Marla Conn, ReadAbility, Inc.

Design: The Design Lab

Photo Credits: Cover and page 3, ©kangshutters/Shutterstock, Inc.; cover inset, ©Holger Wulschlaeger/ Shutterstock, Inc.; page 4, ©Yuriy Rudyy/Shutterstock, Inc.; page 6, ©IM_photo/Shutterstock, Inc.; page 7, ©Mila Semenova/Shutterstock, Inc.; page 9, ©Nickolay Khoroshkov/Shutterstock, Inc.; page 10, ©vagabond54/Shutterstock, Inc.; page 13, ©rickyd/Shutterstock, Inc.; page 14, ©dotshock/Shutterstock, Inc.; page 16, ©Pan Xunbin/Shutterstock, Inc.; page 17, ©Volodymyr Krasyuk/Shutterstock, Inc.; page 19, ©Daleen Loest/Shutterstock, Inc.; page 20, ©PRNewsFoto/Qualcomm MEMS Technologies Inc.; Inventec Corporation; page 21, ©Barnaby Chambers/Shutterstock, Inc; page 23, ©tkemot/Shutterstock, Inc.; page 25, ©Stuart Jenner/Shutterstock, Inc.; page 27, ©Ensuper/Shutterstock, Inc.; page 29, ©Jeff Schultes/Shutterstock, Inc.

Copyright ©2014 by Cherry Lake Publishing
All rights reserved. No part of this book may be reproduced or utilized in any form or by any means without written permission from the publisher

Library of Congress Cataloging-in-Publication Data
Gregory, Josh.
 From butterfly wings to . . . display technology / by Josh Gregory.
    pages cm. — (Innovations from Nature)
 Includes bibliographical references and index.
 ISBN 978-1-62431-754-5 (lib. bdg.) — ISBN 978-1-62431-766-8 (pdf) —
ISBN 978-1-62431-760-6 (pbk.) —ISBN 978-1-62431-772-9 (e-book)
 1. Flat panel displays—Juvenile literature. 2. Butterflies—Juvenile literature.
3. Biomimicry—Juvenile literature. 4. Inventions—Juvenile literature. I. Title.
 TK7882.I6G74 2014
 621.3815'422—dc23   2013030377

Cherry Lake Publishing would like to acknowledge the work of
The Partnership for 21st Century Skills.
Please visit www.p21.org for more information.

Printed in the United States of America
Corporate Graphics Inc.
January 2014

CONTENTS

INNOVATIONS FROM NATURE

CHAPTER ONE

Imitating Nature

Electronic display screens are an important part of most people's everyday routines.

It is very likely that you looked at an electronic display screen sometime recently. Maybe you opened up your laptop this morning to check your e-mail or Twitter. Or perhaps you used your smartphone to send a text message or play your favorite video game. From the portable screens on these devices to the huge screens used for television sets or advertising billboards, electronic displays are almost everywhere we look today.

Display technology is better now than it has ever been. The earliest displays could only show grainy, black-and-white images. They were heavy and expensive. Modern screens are capable of showing incredibly sharp, detailed images using every color the eye can see. You can even carry one in the palm of your hand. However, there is still room for improvement. Some of today's top innovators are working to push display technology even farther.

Throughout history, scientists and **engineers** have worked to create new products and ways of doing things. Some of these inventions, such as medicines and energy sources, have solved major problems in the world. Others, such as household appliances and new modes of transportation, have made life simpler or easier.

The people who create these inventions are amazing innovators. They think creatively and try to look at problems in new ways. Their inspiration for new innovations can come from almost anywhere. Today, more and more scientists and engineers are looking toward nature as a source of ideas for their projects. They examine the way a plant or animal does something. Then they try to duplicate the natural process using the materials and technology available to them. This method of innovating is known as **biomimicry**. Inventions created using biomimicry are often more **sustainable** than traditional inventions. Biomimicry experts hope that their work will enable people to find more natural ways of enjoying modern conveniences without harming the planet.

Inventors have been inspired by nature throughout history. For example, the earliest aircraft were created after people looked to the skies and saw birds soaring through the air. For hundreds of years, inventors worked to build birdlike machines that could carry people high above the ground.

Without inspiration from nature, airplanes would not exist today.

Have you ever noticed that it is more difficult to read an electronic display screen when you are in bright sunlight?

A more recent example of biomimicry is the Mirasol display technology created by the wireless communications company Qualcomm. Have you ever tried to look at a screen on a computer, e-reader, or phone when you are standing outside on a sunny day? It can be hard to read most kinds of display screens in these

Learning & Innovation Skills

 Inventors, scientists, and engineers get inspiration from many different sources. Sometimes they might get an idea for a new invention as they are working on a completely different project. Other times they might come up with ideas for a new device by discussing their thoughts with colleagues. You never know what might give you the idea of a lifetime. If you think creatively, you could be an innovator one day.

conditions. Mirasol screens use a groundbreaking new process called interferometric modulation (IMOD) to display vivid colors in even the brightest sunlight.

The development of this remarkable new technology began when an engineer named Mark Miles read an article about the way butterfly wings reflect sunlight in a special way. This reflection is what creates the wings' bright colors as the insect flutters through the air on a sunny day. Miles realized that this process could provide important clues that might help him create a better kind of display technology. He knew that he would need to not only re-create the butterfly wing's structure using available materials but also find a way to make his invention change colors on command. This would be necessary in order to display different text, images, or animations on the screen. Miles knew that creating such a device would not be simple. He set out to learn everything he could about the unique structure of a butterfly's wing.

CHAPTER TWO

Wondrous Wings

The bright, white light from a lightbulb contains all colors at once.

When you walk into a dark room and flip on the light switch, your eyes are suddenly able to see all of the colorful objects around the room. Have you ever wondered why light allows you to see what color something is?

The visible light that comes from sunlight, flames, or **artificial** light sources is a **wave** that contains all of the different colors an eye can see. As the light waves hit different objects, some parts of the light are **absorbed**. Other parts are **reflected**. When an object appears black, it means that all of the wave was absorbed. It has no color. When an object appears white, it means that all of the wave was reflected. The object is reflecting a combination of all the colors at once. Other colors are displayed when only certain parts of the light wave are reflected.

Most things reflect different colors because they contain different **pigments**. Pigments are materials that reflect light in different ways to create colors. Some

Take a close look at a butterfly's wings to see how they shimmer in the sunlight.

pigments occur naturally. These are the substances that give skin, hair, and other body parts their coloring. Pigments also give color to flowers and other plant parts. Other pigments are created artificially. They are used in paints, dyes, and other substances used to give objects color.

While there is some pigment found in butterfly wings, most of a butterfly's eye-catching appearance comes from something called structural coloring. Structural color can look very different from color that comes from pigments. Have you ever noticed the way a butterfly's wings seems to shimmer and slightly change color as they move through the air? This is called **iridescence**.

Pigments are not iridescent. If you pick up most objects and move them around to reflect light at different angles, they will always stay the same color. Objects that have structural color are iridescent. They appear to change color as they reflect light toward the eye at different angles.

Instead of relying on pigments, objects with structural color reflect light differently based on their shape. A butterfly's wing is formed by a thin, colorless **membrane**. The surface of this membrane is covered with a huge number of extremely tiny scales. Each scale is covered in a pattern of ridges. These ridges are so small that they cannot be seen without using a powerful microscope. However, they are covered in another level of even smaller ridges of their own!

Learning & Innovation Skills

A butterfly's brightly colored wings are not just for show. Their beautiful colors play an important role in the butterfly's survival. Some butterflies are colored in a way that helps them avoid animals that might try to eat them. Their wings might help them blend in with certain kinds of plants or make them look like bigger, more dangerous animals. Some butterflies also use their wings to attract other butterflies when it comes time for them to **mate**.

As light hits a butterfly's wing, these tiny ridges reflect light back like mirrors do. Because the ridges are different sizes and shapes, and pointed in different directions, the light waves they reflect are directed into each other. These colliding light waves are what give the wing its color. Depending on how the waves hit each other, they can be affected in different ways. Some parts of the waves cancel out other parts of the waves they hit. This removes certain colors from the light, leaving others behind for the eye to see. Other parts of the light waves match up and enhance each other. This makes certain colors even brighter. As the butterfly moves, the ridges on its wing scales are tilted at different angles to the light. This is what makes the wings appear iridescent.

Butterflies are not the only animals to display the natural beauty of structural color. For example, bird feathers sometimes have some structural color. Have you ever seen the majestic tail display of a peacock? This large bird's tail feathers can display a wide range of beautiful, iridescent colors thanks to their structure. The shells of certain insects also have structural color. Have you ever seen the way some beetles seem to be green, blue, and black all at the same time? That is an example of structural color.

Can you imagine if the beauty of these colors could be captured and reproduced on the electronic displays you look at every day? Thanks to the latest technological advances, you might not have to wait long before trying out such a screen for yourself.

A peacock's beautiful feathers are just one example of structural color.

CHAPTER THREE

From the Skies to the Screen

Most flat screen TVs use LCD screens.

Most of today's electronic displays rely on liquid crystal display (LCD) technology. An LCD display screen is made up of pieces called **pixels**. Modern screens can contain several million of these tiny objects. Each pixel contains pigments in three colors: red, blue, and green. These three colors can be combined in different ways to form every other color the eye can see.

An LCD screen sends electrical signals into its pixels. This electricity makes each pixel on the screen rearrange its pigments to form a certain color. As the electrical signal changes, the pixels change colors. This causes new images to appear on the screen.

You have probably noticed that you can see most LCD screens perfectly fine even in a completely dark room. In fact, LCD screens are often easier to read in dim light than they are under bright lights. This is because they do not rely on reflected waves of light. Instead, each LCD screen has a backlight. This is a light source that shines outward from behind the screen. As the light from the backlight passes through the screen's pixels, it takes on their color before reaching your eyes.

The outer surface of an LCD screen is often made of glass or some other transparent substance. This makes it easy for your eyes to see the colored pixels of the screen. However, these surfaces are often very reflective. As white light from the sun or a lamp reflects off the surface of the screen, it blends with the colored light waves coming from the backlight. This makes the screen's colors look dull and difficult to see.

IMOD displays solve this issue by using a type of structural coloring system. Underneath an IMOD screen's clear outer covering there are millions of tiny plates arranged between two reflective membranes.

Each plate is too small to see without using a microscope. These plates are similar to pixels. However, they do not contain pigments. Instead, they move around to form reflective shapes that are similar to the ridges on the scales of a butterfly wing.

When an IMOD screen is powered on, it sends an electrical signal to the plates that causes them to draw together into an arrangement that absorbs all light. This makes the screen appear black. As the screen's device

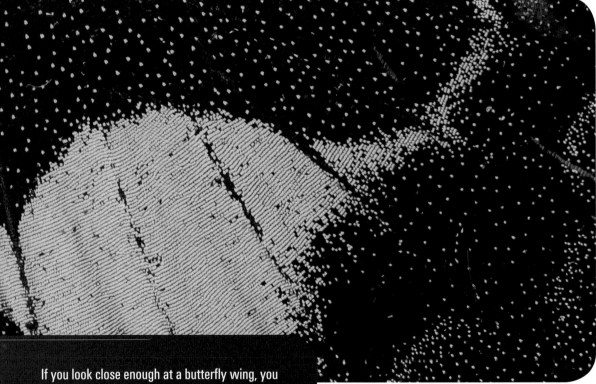

If you look close enough at a butterfly wing, you can see the individual scales that cover it.

You can also see individual pixels if you look close enough at an LCD screen.

21st Century Content

 **LCD screens require far more electricity to work than IMOD screens do. This means that IMOD screens are much better for the environment. In recent decades, more and more people have become aware of the damage that excessive energy use can cause to the environment. As a result, they try to avoid being wasteful. Environmentally friendly products such as IMOD screens are becoming quite popular. Many of tomorrow's greatest innovations will be based around products that people can use without harming the world we live in.**

needs to display different images, it sends electrical signals that cause the plates to arrange into new formations. These formations leave different sizes of gaps in between the plates. As light passes through these gaps, parts of it are absorbed and parts are reflected, just as it is when it hits the surface of a butterfly wing. The light that is reflected from an IMOD screen comes back in different colors, causing an image to display on the screen.

Just as the color of a butterfly's wing seems to change slightly as it catches light at different angles, the plates in an IMOD screen move back and forth to reflect light at different angles. This movement causes reflected light to change colors. The plates in the screen can move very quickly. This means that the image on the screen can appear to be changing almost constantly. This fast change in colors allows the screen to display smooth, realistic videos and animations just as well as an LCD screen can.

With the ability to display sharp, colorful video without a backlight, IMOD could very well become the standard for electronic displays.

Backlights allow you to read tablets and other LCD displays even when a room is completely dark.

CHAPTER FOUR

A Colorful Future

This phone uses a version of Qualcomm's IMOD technology.

IMOD displays are cutting-edge technology. They are so new, in fact, that they aren't available for people to purchase yet. The engineers at Qualcomm have created functioning versions of the screens, but they are still working to perfect them for use in a variety of devices.

IMOD screens offer many advantages over other types of screens that are used in devices today. For instance,

IMOD devices can save electricity by being charged less often than other electronics.

LCD screens need backlights in order to be seen. As a result, they require a constant source of electricity to power their lights. IMOD displays need only electricity to move the plates in the screen when the image changes. This means they do not require nearly as much power.

Life & Career Skills

No one knows yet whether IMOD screens will become popular with customers. Just because something is a good idea does not mean people will want to buy it. Some great devices are simply too expensive for most people to afford. Other times, a company is unable to convince shoppers that its new product offers advantages over the competition. Even if an invention does not succeed at first, however, it might catch on at a later time. Or it might inspire another innovator to create an even better version!

Because they use less electricity, IMOD devices can be used for a long time before their batteries need to be recharged. The inventors believe that their screens will be able to go for days or even weeks between battery charges. This would make IMOD devices very useful for travelers and others who might not always have access to electrical outlets when they need them. A lack of a backlight also makes IMOD screens thinner than LCD displays. This means they can be used to create even smaller, more portable devices.

Because IMOD screens do not use backlights, they are easier on the eyes than LCD screens. Have you ever tried to read a long book or magazine on a tablet computer or a laptop monitor? After a while, you might notice your eyes getting tired. This is because of the bright backlight that is shining into them. Your eyes are more comfortable when they are looking at light that is reflecting off of something. For example, think of the pages of a printed book.

Words are printed onto paper using pigments, and you can comfortably read them for hours at a time. IMOD screens have a similar effect on the eyes.

Some devices, such as e-readers, use a type of screen called E Ink. Like an IMOD screen, an E Ink screen is reflective and very easy to read for long periods of time. It can also be read in direct, bright light. However, E Ink

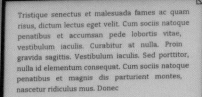

E ink screens are used in e-reader devices because they do not strain the eyes as much as LCD screens do.

screens rely on pigments instead of structural color. It takes much longer for an E Ink screen to change the arrangement of its pigments than it does for an IMOD screen to rearrange its plates. This is not a problem when it comes to displaying text. However, this drawback prevents E Ink screens from displaying videos or animations like IMOD screens can.

E-readers will likely be some of the first devices released with IMOD displays. However, if the new technology is a hit, it might be used in many more types of devices. The small screens on digital cameras, cell phones, and wristwatches might one day make use of IMOD technology. Huge TVs and outdoor billboards could also benefit from IMOD's advantages. Some people even believe that IMOD could one day replace pigment-based paints. Imagine being able to flip a switch and change the color of a room's walls. Or perhaps you could add a design to the top of your desk and then change the design when you got tired of it. The possibilities are almost limitless.

It remains to be seen whether IMOD will be a success. Only time will tell if its abilities are the sort of thing that people want in a new product. But no matter how successful it ends up being, there is no question that the technology behind IMOD is impressive. To think that it all started with a butterfly wing shimmering in the sunlight. Once again, biomimicry has led to an incredible innovation.

CHAPTER FIVE

Daring Display Developers

Electronic display screens have gone through a lot of changes since they were first invented. It has taken the combined work of many different innovators over the course of decades to bring us the advanced display technology that is used widely today. Here are some of the most important innovators in the history of display screens.

The display screens we use every day would not exist without the hard work of past innovators.

Life & Career Skills

Engineering is a fascinating scientific field and one worth considering as a career choice. An engineer is a problem solver who uses his or her knowledge in many different areas—including aerospace, mining, computers, electronics, agriculture, architecture, and other fields. Engineers are required to exercise a high degree of creativity and innovative thinking. Engineers are often highly paid. If you choose a career in engineering, you'll most likely be challenged to push your talents to their limit, and you will have the chance to make the world a better place through your hard work.

Karl Ferdinand Braun (1850–1918) was born in Germany. After earning a doctorate in physics from the University of Berlin, he began working as a professor and conducting his own experiments. In 1897, he created the first cathode ray tube (CRT) display screen. The screen emitted light when it was struck from behind with electrical signals from the tube inside. Advanced versions of the technology were later used to create the first television sets and computer monitors.

James Fergason (1934–2008) was born and raised in Missouri. He attended college at the University of Missouri, where he studied physics and became interested in a type of substance called a liquid crystal. Liquid crystals have properties of both liquids and solids at the same time. After graduating, Fergason went to work at a research laboratory in Pennsylvania,

The cathode ray tube was once used in all television screens.

where he began searching for uses for liquid crystals.
In the 1960s, he joined the Liquid Crystal Institute
in Ohio, where he soon discovered how liquid crystals

Life & Career Skills

Despite being highly intelligent and forward-thinking innovators, Mark Miles, Karl Ferdinand Braun, and James Fergason did not come up with their creations all on their own. They relied on help from fellow researchers, engineers, and scientists to help them develop their ideas into finished creations. They also built on the knowledge gathered by previous inventors. For example, Miles could not have gotten an idea for a new type of display if displays had never been invented in the first place!

could be used to build display screens. Fergason's discoveries have been the foundation of LCD development since then.

Mark Miles first came up with the idea for IMOD screens while reading an article about butterfly wings in a science magazine. He began thinking about how he could imitate the butterfly's structural color and what uses such technology would have. Before long, he realized that structural color would be useful for display screens. He started a company called Iridigm to research his ideas and develop the new technology. In 2004, Qualcomm was so impressed with Iridigm's work that it bought the company for $170 million and turned its work into the Mirasol project.

If a butterfly can inspire a whole new type of display technology, there's no telling what biomimicry will produce next!

Glossary

absorbed (ab-ZORBD) soaked up

artificial (ahr-tuh-FISH-uhl) made by people rather than existing in nature

biomimicry (bye-oh-MI-mi-kree) the practice of studying and copying nature's forms and systems to solve human problems

engineers (en-juh-NIRZ) people who are specially trained to design and build things

iridescence (ear-uh-DESS-uhnss) the characteristic of some surfaces to change color when viewed from different angles

mate (MAYT) to join together to produce babies

membrane (MEM-brane) a very thin layer of tissue

pigments (PIG-muhnts) substances that give color to something

pixels (PIKS-uhlz) tiny dots that make up the visual image on a display screen

reflected (ri-FLEK-tid) thrown back from a surface

sustainable (suh-STAY-nuh-buhl) done in a way that can be continued and that doesn't use up natural resources

wave (WAYV) an amount of energy that travels through air or water in the shape of a wave, as in sound waves or light waves

For More Information

BOOKS

Gorman, John. *Light: An Investigation*. New York: PowerKids Press, 2008.

Murawski, Darlyne. *Face to Face with Butterflies*. Washington, DC: National Geographic, 2010.

WEB SITES

Biomimicry 3.8—Case Examples
http://biomimicry.net/about/biomimicry/case-examples/
Learn more about some of the amazing innovations that biomimicry has inspired.

Qualcomm—Mirasol
www.qualcomm.com/mirasol/benefits
Learn more about Qualcomm's Mirasol IMOD displays.

Index

About the Author

Josh Gregory writes and edits books for kids. He lives in Chicago, Illinois.

JUN   2015   2 1982 02858 0821